Of Smoke & Mirrors

Investigating Earth's Geothermal Phenomena

Table of Contents

Chapter 1. Introduction

Beneath the surface of our everyday world teems a realm of hidden power and mystifying forces, driving the essential cycles of the Earth - its geothermal phenomena. Our special report, "Of Smoke & Mirrors: Investigating Earth's Geothermal Phenomena," journey through this labyrinth of subterranean wonders, at times mystifying, at other times intimidating, yet improbably imbricated within our existence. But fret not, we won't embroil you in layers of inscrutable technical jargon. In the following pages, we unfurl the many secrets concealed beneath our feet with clarity and flair, digestible for anyone fascinated by the world's natural wonders. From geyser eruptions and geothermal energy, right down to hot springs and tectonic activity - we take you on a riveting sojourn beneath the Earth's surface. If you're a lover of Planet Earth, this special report is an adventure not to be missed!

Chapter 2. Introduction to Earth's Hidden Powerhouse

Down below, deeper than most of us can fathom, lie unseen forces hard at work, spinning Earth's awe-inspiring cycles. The Earth's subsurface, marked by these geothermal phenomena, forms a veritable powerhouse, giving rise to dramatic and stupefying manifestations that enchant our minds incessantly.

2.1. Delving Deep into Earth's Interior

The Earth's interior is a mammoth, white-hot incinerator, churning with relentless intensity. Towards the centre, temperatures spiral upwards, sometimes breaching a staggering 5700 degrees Celsius - hotter than the surface of the sun. The nature of Earth's core behoves us to unravel the intricacies of these enormous temperatures.

The Earth's interior, primarily segregated into three layers: your immediate acquaintance, the crust; the expansive mantle; and the elusive, enigmatic core. The crust, which hosts our seas, continents, and lives, is understandably the chilliest part. Subsequent inward, the temperature increases progressively.

Each of these layers is accentuated by their unique concoction of elements. The density of the materials aids these layers in claiming their designated spots inside the Earth. Luminary metals like iron and nickel, due to their density, predominantly make home in the core.

2.2. Power beneath Our Feet: The Source

As we delve deeper, weariness morphs into wonder. The mantle, underpinning the crust, lends itself to the Earth's character. Laden with molten rocks metamorphosing and writhing, the mantle is a testament to Earth's dynamism. The temperatures here are homogenous, fluctuating around 1000 - 1200 degrees Celsius.

The mantle is where the Earth's untamed power resides. Stirred by the immense heat from the core and the relatively cooler regions of the crust, dense materials in the mantle plunge into the depths, only to be replaced by the buoyant, less dense material spiraling up. Thus ensues a colossal conveyor belt effect, better known as mantle convection.

The Earth's powerhouse reciprocates the sun's blazing energy with its life-fostering warmth, courtesy of this radioactive decay and mantle convection.

2.3. Geothermal Gradients: A Heat Perspective

The gradient of temperature rise as we progress into Earth's depths forms the Geothermal Gradient. Traditionally, the geothermal gradient is asserted as a 25-30 degrees Celsius increase for every kilometer of depth, with some perturbations triggered by local geological structures and anomalies.

This gradient is steadfast; where the outer layers of the crust might be buffeted by seasonal changes, the deeper realms stay unwavering, harboring a relatively constant temperature. Try visualizing the Earth with its exterior, showing changing seasons and internal states of fluctuating stability - it's almost akin to a large, simmering apple pie.

2.4. The Reservoirs of Heat: Geothermal Reserves

We've walked you through the dynamics of heat generation beneath the surface. But where, you might ask, is this heat stationed? The answer lies in the Earth's geothermal reservoirs.

Found at an assortment of depths, these reservoirs can vary dramatically in size and temperature. Essential phenomena like plate tectonic activity, magma movements, and seismic activity act as catalysts creating these heat repositories. These geothermal reserves are often caged within fluid-filled porous rocks, enabling extraction.

2.5. The Unseen Force: Geothermal Energy

This vast quantity of Earth's heat forms the keystone for geothermal energy - an unfathomable resource of power readily available, should we effectively harness it.

Geothermal energy, the Earth's generous gift, encapsulates heat energy generated and stored within the Earth's lithosphere. This terrestrial energy cascades through the open wounds of the Earth's crust, through its volcanoes, hot springs, and geysers booming with gaseous energy. Yet, it's not confined exclusively to these portal zones; beneath us, every step we thread is a vault of repressed heat - a beacon of colossal potential.

2.6. The Earth as a Natural Dynamo

Earth's power beneath the crust is not only about heat; it also concerns the motion of this heat. The fluidic outer core of the Earth, when set into motion by the scorching heat from the core interfacing with the relatively cooler mantle, generates innate electric currents. These currents transform the Earth into a natural dynamo, yielding the planet's magnetic field, an invaluable shield deflecting harmful cosmic radiation.

This labyrinth of powers intertwined forms an intricate dance that, while concealed from the naked eye, has far-reaching implications above ground. From even modest stirrings beneath, the ramifications are tremendous, evidenced in monumental events like earthquakes, volcanic eruptions, and the creation of exotic geothermal formations.

In conclusion, the unassuming beneath of the Earth hosts a throbbing powerhouse, unsung yet omnipotent. The geothermal phenomena residing deep in the Earth's mantle personify an ancient global engine - ceaseless, enigmatic, and utterly crucial. The expansive mantle beneath our feet, along with its dynamic convective behemoths, renders the Earth its own stellar dynamo, an oasis of power concealed in the depth, humming with silent vitality, spinning the wheel of the world as we know it.

Chapter 3. Unearthing the Secrets beneath the Crust

Delving deep into the Earth's crust, we find ourselves in a world filled with dynamic processes and interactive elements. This zone, which expands from the Earth's exterior down to about 40 kilometers in depth, harbors a mysterious realm of constantly morphing conditions. Geological activities such as volcanic eruptions, earthquakes, mountain formation, and the creation of our beautiful seas all trace back to the life beneath the crust.

3.1. The Anatomy of the Earth's Crust:

The Earth's crust, a relatively thin, rocky layer, encloses our abode. Constituted mainly of quartz and silicates, its actual thickness varies considerably, from about 5-10 kilometers beneath the oceans (oceanic crust) to about 30-50 kilometers underneath our continents (continental crust). The latter, often compared to buoyant icebergs floating in denser molten rock, contains the highest mountains and the deepest mines. As we delve deeper, we encounter the boundary between the crust and the mantle, the Mohorovicic Discontinuity, named after the Croatian seismologist who unearthed this phenomenon.

3.2. Crust: A Playground of Plate Tectonics:

Underneath the crust exists the curious world of plate tectonics. Propelled by the roiling, convective heat engine of the Earth's deeper levels, dozens of relatively thin lithospheric slabs constantly move, albeit at a glacial pace. This movement leads to the interactions known as plate tectonics, which manifest in three ways:

- Divergent Boundaries: These areas, where plates pull away from each other like rift valleys or undersea ridges, witness magma from the mantle coursing to the surface, generating new crust.

- Convergent Boundaries: Here, plates gravitate towards each other. The denser, usually oceanic one plunges back into the mantle, a process known as 'subduction.' This can spur seismic and volcanic activities.

- Transformation Boundaries: Plates in these zones slide past each other. One such famous instance is the San Andreas Fault in California.

Plate tectonic activities further influence climate and even life evolution.

3.3. Strength Within: The Economic Value of the Crust:

Hidden within the crust is a treasure trove of natural resources, fueling the engines of human civilization. We find ores of countless metals essential to modern life: copper for our electronics, iron for cars and skyscrapers, aluminium for our aircraft, and even rarer elements like gold and diamonds.

Geothermal energy, especially, holds the limelight for its potential in future energy requirements. Here, heat from the molten core ascends towards the crust, which we then convert to electricity. It offers a renewable, relatively clean source of power that could contribute significantly to a sustainable future.

3.4. The Secrets of Geothermal Phenomena:

Deep within the Earth's crust, a relentless geological process is underway. The radioactive decay from uranium, thorium, and potassium present heats up the mantle, fostering a breathtaking range of geothermal phenomena. Iconic ones include:

- Volcanoes: With the molten rock – or magma – pent up in the mantle, volcanoes are the Earth's way of venting out excess heat.

- Geysers: These showstoppers of the geothermal world are fountains of water erupting from the ground, often accompanied by steam. Their unique behavior is due to specific conditions underground.

- Hot Springs: Typically associated with volcanic regions, hot springs occur when groundwaters heated by geothermal energy find their way to the surface.

- Fumaroles: These openings in Earth's crust release steam and volcanic gases, often creating a mood of eerie desolation.

3.5. The Impact and Importance of Geothermal Phenomena:

Undoubtedly, geothermal phenomena profoundly shape life on Earth, playing roles far beyond offering awe-inspiring spectacles. They feed the soil with nutrients, raise islands from the sea, shape the landscapes and even influence the carbon cycle - a critical element of life on Earth.

We may often overlook the importance of the crust in our daily lives. We see it as a mere solid foundation, bearing our weight while sheltering us from the planet's fiery interior. However, the crust not only shields but also transports vital thermal energy from the depths to the surface, regulating temperatures, driving geological processes and enabling life.

In many ways, the crust is akin to a mysterious book, narrating the Earth's past and present and projecting a window onto its potential future. As we further scrutinize its cryptic verses, we not only untangle the secrets of our planet but also learn how to navigate the challenges and opportunities it presents.

Understanding these geothermal phenomena and harnessing their power could significantly contribute to our civilization. They underpin the potential for renewable energy, provide insights into climate change, and propel us towards a more sustainable, resilient future. Through this understanding, we can encourage a harmonious interplay between the Earth's fiery core and the surface, thereby preserving the balance of our natural world.

Chapter 4. The Telling Tale of Tectonic Plates

In the symphony of natural forces that compose our Earth, the movement of tectonic plates might very well serve as the grand conductor. Yet, despite orchestrating such awesome phenomena as earthquakes, volcanic activity, and the very creation of mountain ranges, these gargantuan slabs of solid rock often move no faster than the growth rate of human fingernails. It's a reminder of the unfathomable scales at which geology operates, where even slow movements can translate into profound changes given the luxury of millions of years.

4.1. The Birth of the Plate Tectonics Theory

The theory of plate tectonics, despite lying at the heart of modern geology, is a relatively recent development. It was not until the 1960s, building upon the hypotheses of continental drift and seafloor spreading, that the concept of Earth's crust being divided into large plates gained acceptance.

The shapes of continents sparked curiosity among early cartographers, who noticed that the eastern coastline of South America and the western coastline of Africa seemed like puzzle pieces that could fit together. An early 20th-century German meteorologist, Alfred Wegener, proposed the theory of continental drift to explain this, suggesting that the continents had once been jammed together into a supercontinent - the 'Pangaea'. With time, they had drifted apart to create the modern Earth's face.

Despite the striking visual evidence, Wegener was not immediately embraced by fellow scientists due to the lack of a persuasive mechanism that could push the continents apart. It is this missing piece that the theory of seafloor spreading offered. The hypothesis, proposed by Harry Hess and Robert Dietz in the early 1960s, suggested new oceanic crust was being formed at mid-oceanic ridges, pushing the older crust outwards.

The advent of technologies that allowed scientists to study the ocean floor and remote geologic formations helped to solidify these theories into the current model of plate tectonics.

4.2. The Structure Below

When we talk of tectonic plates, we refer to the Earth's lithosphere - a rigid outer layer that envelops our planet like an eggshell. This uppermost layer of the Earth's mantle, donned with the Earth's crust, is what comprises these gigantic plates. Yet, hidden beneath this solid veneer is the asthenosphere, the partially molten upper layer of the mantle, where enormous pressures and temperatures create a tumult of slow-moving rocks. It is upon this pliable layer that the tectonic plates surf.

Beneath the ocean bed, these plates are relatively thin, perhaps only 5 kilometers thick, comprised chiefly of dense basalt. The continents, however, rest on significantly thicker plates, of the order of 30-50 kilometers, composed of less dense granite.

There are seven major and many minor plates, the largest being the Pacific Plate, which underlies the vast Pacific Ocean.

4.3. The Dance of the Tectonic Plates

Tectonic plates do not stay still. They are in constant, albeit slow, movement, propelled by the convective currents of the underlying mantle. Sea floor spreading at the mid-ocean ridges pushes the plates apart, while in other areas, plates crash into one another, one being forced under its rival in a process known as subduction. Occasionally, plates slide past each other laterally, creating transform boundaries.

This tectonic dance spells out a dramatic cycle - the Wilson Cycle - that begins with the creation of new oceanic plate material at mid-ocean ridges, the growth and eventual closing of oceans, and the collision of continental plates leading to the formation of mountains.

4.4. Tectonic Plates and Their Impacts

The movements of tectonic plates dramatically impact the Earth. They could gradually create towering mountains, such as the Himalayas, and deep ocean trenches, like the Marianas. This slow tectonic ballet also triggers a wealth of hazardous events with immediate consequences - earthquakes, tsunamis, and volcanic eruptions.

The power unleashed during these events can be terrifying, yet it is this very interplay of forces that has sculpted our world into the diverse, dynamic, and beautiful entity it is today.

To fully grasp how geology has shaped our Earth's past and will continue to forge its future, we have to delve into the slow rhythm of the planet's pulse - the shifting and grinding of its tectonic plates. Such understanding grants us an appreciation of not only the geological phenomena around us, but the fragile place of life within this grand, geological theatre. It indeed is a tale of multi-layered intricacy and far-reaching ramifications - truly an epic beneath our feet.

Chapter 5. Gushers of Steam: Understanding Geysers

Just below our feet, an awe-inspiring spectacle unfolds sporadically. With an unexpected roar and burst, steam and boiling water gush into the sky, creating an impressive display that enthralls any passing observer. This phenomenon, known as geyser eruption, is simultaneously perplexing, stunning and, to the scientist, an intellectual enigma inviting exploration. Yet, the processes that give rise to this spectacle remain beneath the Earth surface, concealed by layers of rock, and shrouded in intrigue.

5.1. The Making of a Geyser

Understanding the formation of a geyser requires a journey deep into the Earth's crust. In essence, a geyser is a hot spring with peculiar plumbing that allows it to periodically erupt. They are formed where there's a combination of water, heat, and the appropriate underlying geology. The Earth's mantle, resplendent with molten rock called magma, heats the underground rocks and the water that seeped into the ground.

This water, subjected to the Earth's internal heat, begins to warm and eventually reaches boiling point. However, the immense pressure exerted on it by the overlying water and rocks prevents it from turning into vapor instantaneously, and instead, it remains in a superheated state.

Ordinarily, the heated water would rise buoyantly towards the surface. But the peculiar geological structure that funnels into narrow fractures or tubes in the rocks impedes its free passage. This forms a natural valve system that traps a portion of the water underground.

Meanwhile, the heat continues to transform more and more water into its gaseous state, increasing the pressure on the trapped water column. When the pressure becomes unbearably high, it forces the superheated water upwards, hurling it out of the ground in a spectacular eruption. As the water is expelled, the pressure drops, and the steam condenses back into water, allowing the geyser to reset for its next display.

5.2. The Lifeblood of Geysers: Water

For a geyser to form, the necessity of an ample water supply cannot be overstated. The water seeping into the ground can come from a variety of sources, including rain, melting snow, or underground springs. Water's role as a geothermal courier can't be overstated; it transports the Earth's internal heat to the surface, creating the fantastical performance of the geyser's eruption.

This water percolates down through the ground until it reaches a depth where surrounding rocks are hot enough but not molten. Here, heat transfer begins, slowly raising the water's temperature. But the journey of water is not just a mere descent and ascent; it is interwoven with complex geothermal processes.

Chapter 6. Thermal Power: The Heat Source

At the heart of a geyser's operation is a constant supply of heat. The heat source is typically a magma chamber relatively close to the Earth's surface. Its proximity is paramount; if it were too deep, the water wouldn't reach the necessary temperatures. Conversely, if magma was too near or intersected the water channel, the resultant excessive heat could lead to an explosive volcanic activity instead of a geyser.

The energy stored in the magma is transmitted through the surrounding rocks by conduction, the process that fuels the remarkable geothermal phenomena such as geysers.

6.1. Intricate Plumbing: The Geyser's Geological Structure

Moreover, the presence of an exceptionally structured conduit system is also vital – it is this intricate 'plumbing' that distinguishes a geyser from a common hot spring. The conduit system often comprises layers of permeable and impermeable rock. The former permits passage of water, while the latter acts as a barrier, confining the superheated water and steam below the surface.

The upper regions of the reservoir channel are often clogged with silica-rich deposits called sinter, further narrowing the path to the surface and adding to the pressure. It is, in essence, a pressure cooker that explodes when the internal pressure exceeds its limit.

6.2. The Cycle of an Eruption

A geyser's eruption isn't a singular, isolated event but part of an ongoing cycle. The cycle commences with the "recharge" phase, where water begins to refill the reservoir after an eruption. This period varies from one geyser to another. Some take mere minutes, while others may take hours or even days.

During this period, the underlying heat source begins to reheat the accumulated water. Gradually, the bottom of the water column starts to boil, producing steam bubbles. However, the overlying pressure from the water above restricts the steam from rapidly expanding and venting to the surface. Instead, it gradually ascends, heating the overlying water column. The resulting feedback loop increases the pressure in the geyser's conduit until it is so great that an eruption is triggered, and the cycle is ready to restart.

In a nutshell, geysers are as much a product of their unique environment as they are a marvel of natural thermal science. They are profound reminders of the power and dynamism that constantly churns beneath the solid ground beneath our feet. Their sporadic, dramatic bursts are indeed an exposition of nature's steam-powered artistry written across the Earth's geothermal canvas.

Chapter 7. Therapeutic Soaks: The Science of Hot Springs

Beyond the spectacle of gushing geysers and beneath the relentless thrumming of geothermal power stations are quieter spectacles of the Earth's geothermal dance. Here, the earth exhales balmy whispers from its crust into natural baths known as hot springs. A sanctuary for weary bodies and rejuvenation seekers, these hot springs are sheer proof of the geothermal phenomena operating beneath us, while their healing properties offer enchanting interplays between science and wellness.

7.1. Formation: Geological Orchestra

The formation of hot springs is a symphony performed by the geological orchestra beneath the earth's crust. It begins with precipitation, where rainwater seeps underground, trickling towards the heart of our planet. Deep down, geothermal heat warms the water. This heated water, lighter than the cooler groundwater, rises back to the surface. The location of these springs often corresponds with volcanic activity or fractures and cracks in the Earth's crust, through which the warmed water finds its path back up.

However, a hot spring's temperature is directly influenced by the geothermal gradient, not merely the presence of a nearby volcano. The geothermal gradient refers to the increasing temperature with depth into the Earth. Shaped by the local geology and Earth's inner heat, the gradient varies widely, determining the temperature of these delightful springs.

Hard rock underground layers can channel this heated water considerable distances, maintaining its heat due to the rock's insulating capacities. This process results in thermal springs appearing in places unexpected, sometimes far from obvious volcanic activity.

7.2. Mineral Content: Earth's Healing Potions

Each hot spring holds a complex cocktail of minerals. Although the exact composition varies, a hot spring's healing reputation is often anchored in this unique mineral mixture. The water's journey through the Earth means it erodes mineral-rich rocks, consequently imbuing the water with compounds such as silica, magnesium, calcium, and even rarer elements like radium or lithium.

The skin, when soaking in this nutrient-rich water, can absorb these minerals, offering potential health benefits. Magnesium, for instance, may aid blood circulation, while sulfate can soothe achy muscles. Further, the heat itself can stimulate peripheral blood flow and promote detoxification. However, it's essential to remember that while many springs are rich in beneficial compounds, others can contain substances that are hazardous at high concentrations.

7.3. Therapeutic Benefits: Nature's Spa

Long before the advent of modern spa treatments, civilizations worldwide recognized hot springs' therapeutic potential. Beyond pain relief, these springs have been associated with several health benefits, from improving skin health to reducing stress and promoting sound sleep.

The warm water can work on multiple levels - physically relaxing the muscles, removing toxins, improving circulation, and activating the body's natural healing powers. On a psychological level, sitting in nature's hot tub, surrounded often by serene landscapes, can provide an incredible boost to mental well-being.

Epsom salt hot springs, rich in magnesium and sulfate, are renowned for reducing inflammation and relieving muscle aches. Sulfur springs, although distinctive in their odor, are celebrated for treating skin diseases like psoriasis, dermatitis, and fungal infections. Meanwhile, springs rich in radium, despite their trace radioactive content, can offer significant pain relief for arthritis sufferers.

While the scientific community rightly advises caution until more research is conducted, the anecdotes of health and healing from hot spring bathers across centuries are compelling testimonials to these geothermal phenomena.

7.4. Hot Springs Around the World: A Jacuzzi Tour

The astonishing aspect of these geothermal gifts is their global distribution. From Japan's 'Onsen' to Turkey's 'Pamukkale,' or Iceland's geothermal lagoon 'Blue Lagoon,' these hot springs cross cultural and geographical boundaries. Each region harbors hot springs through distinct geological activities and possesses a unique combination of minerals.

Hot springs are also repositories of cultural stories and historical anecdotes. Bathing rituals, traditional medicine, and social customs are often intertwined with these natural phenomena, providing a glimpse into a community's broader context.

7.5. The Power Beneath: Conservation and Caution

Despite the diverse benefits of hot springs, it is vital to also recognize their delicate nature. Over-commercialization and careless usage threaten these geothermal wonders, and our very presence can inadvertently lead to their degradation. Mismanagement can lead to water contamination, temperature changes, or even spring extinction. There is a need for balancing the exploitative tendencies with sustainable practices.

Just as tricky is the need for caution while using hot springs as a health remedy. Hot springs undoubtedly possess potential wellness properties, but their use should always be accompanied by sound medical advice. The healing earth gives us must not turn into inadvertent poisoning.

7.6. Conclusion: Embracing Earth's Generosity

The hot springs or nature's open-air Jacuzzis are more than just geothermal phenomena - they embody Earth's generosity and a delicate merging of science and wellness. They are places where the wonders of Earth's interior surges to the surface, offering us a bath both literally and metaphorically in the planet's complex systems. But as we embrace these soothing offerings, it is paramount we do so astride respect and awareness for their preservation and our safety. Enjoying these sanctuaries responsibly ensures they continue to inspire, heal, and enrich lives for millennia to come.

Chapter 8. Harnessing Heat: The Mechanics of Geothermal Energy

Geothermal energy leverages the inherent heat from the Earth's crust, converting it into usable electrical power. It's the unseen force beneath our feet, a pandora box of untapped capacity that, once fully harnessed, promises to power up our existence in unimaginable scales. In our journey to deconstruct this underground marvel, let's first uncover the roots of geothermal energy.

8.1. The Genesis of Geothermal Energy

The Earth's core, despite being over 4,000 miles beneath the surface, can reach temperatures hotter than the surface of the sun. Heat radiates from the core, warming the surrounding mantle, a thick layer of molten rock known as magma. A small fraction of this magma rises through the Earth's lithosphere — the solid outer section of our planet, composed of the crust and the uppermost portion of the mantle. The heated magma and rocks in the lithosphere transfer their heat to ground water, resulting in underground reservoirs of hot water and steam. This, in essence, forms the geothermal energy that we are equipped to harness.

8.2. Geothermal Power Plants: Unleashing the Beast

Geothermal power plants employ three different methods to convert geothermal energy into electrical power: Dry Steam, Flash Steam, and Binary Cycle.

Dry Steam Power Plants

These are the oldest type of geothermal power plants, first established in Italy in 1904. Dry steam plants directly use the steam from underground reservoirs to turn turbine generators. Post energy generation, the used steam is discharged into the atmosphere.

Flash Steam Power Plants

More commonly found, flash steam plants take high-pressure hot water from the ground and convert it into steam to run generator turbines. Once the steam cools, it condenses back to water and is returned to the ground to replenish the reservoir.

Binary Cycle Power Plants

The binary cycle power plants represent the newest breed. In these, the heat from geothermal water is transferred to a secondary liquid with a lower boiling point, causing it to vaporize. The vapor runs the generators, and post process, both the vapor and the geothermal water are returned to the earth, posing minimal harm to the environment.

8.3. Hydrothermal Fields and Enhanced Geothermal Systems

Geothermal power plants generally depend upon hydrothermal fields, areas with high heat flow coupled with an abundance of ground water. These fields are typically found near tectonic plate boundaries where volcanic activity is prominent. However, such regions limit the global applications of geothermal energy, leading scientists to extract heat through Enhanced Geothermal Systems (EGS).

EGS entails drilling deep into the Earth's crust, fracturing the rock, and pumping water into the fractures to generate steam. Although EGS offers a way to exploit geothermal energy anywhere on Earth, it's use is still in experimental stages, and commercial use so far remains limited due to high initiation costs and various operational challenges.

8.4. The Sweet and the Sour: Advantages and Disadvantages

Like every alternative energy source, geothermal energy has its advantages and disadvantages. It's renewable and reliable, providing virtually limitless energy source with a consistent output unaffected by weather conditions. Geothermal power plants also have lower emissions compared to conventional fossil fuel power plants, making them a cleaner energy option.

However, harnessing geothermal energy can also trigger seismic activity, a phenomenon known as induced seismicity. Additionally, though geothermal plants emit less greenhouse gases, some harmful gases can escape during drilling. The capital costs are also high, and site-specific geological studies are necessary before a plant can be established.

8.5. The Future of Geothermal Energy

With increasing focus on renewable energy sources, the future of geothermal energy seems promising. Advancements in technology and methods can overcome some of the existing limitations. Additionally, the prospect of using lower temperature sources through binary cycle power plants and further development in EGS can expand the range and the reach of geothermal energy.

Our Earth, a giant power station, secretively radiates voluminous heat, providing us with an untapped massive reservoir of renewable energy. As we delve deeper beneath the Earth's crust, the promise of a sustainable future gradually comes alive powered by the colossal furnace beneath us. Geothermal power, from its humble inception at the start of the 20th century, stands today on the brink of becoming a giant stride towards a greener tomorrow.

Chapter 9. Volcanoes: A Window into Earth's Fiery Core

Every blaze, every puff of smoke, every tremble beneath our feet, is a tangible manifestation of Earth's ethereal core, literally earth-shaking and dramatically underscoring our planet's ongoing, dynamic transformations. Volcanoes, the natural features that dramatically punctuate these transformations, represent not just destruction and chaos, but also creation, rebirth, and a fascinating side of our living planet.

9.1. The Making of a Volcano

Volcanoes were not magically sculpted overnight, nor are they the byproduct of deliberate intersection between humans and nature. Instead, they have been millions of years in the making, a spectacular testament to Earth's geothermal phenomena. The Earth's molten core, mantle, and crust work cohesively, caught in an inconceivably large-scale cycle of creation and destruction, to produce these colossal natural wonders.

Volcanoes burgeon where the Earth's tectonic plates convolute, demarcating the boundaries of these gargantuan pieces of Earth's crust. At these junctures, enormous pressure and heat slowly nudge magma (molten rock bridging elements such as silicon, oxygen, aluminum, iron, and magnesium) from the Earth's lower crust and upper mantle to ascend towards the surface.

The Earth's crust unknowingly harbors this escalating pressure, providing a fertile crescent for a burgeoning volcano. When the pressure becomes insurmountable, usually over thousands of years, it leads to an eruption—a breath of fresh magma expelled from a fissure on the Earth's surface—which embarks on the process of forming a volcano.

9.2. Anatomy of a Volcano

Understanding the structure of volcanoes provides a clearer comprehension of their creation and destructive capacities. There are three essential parts that can be carried across many types of volcanoes: the magma chamber, the conduit, and the vent.

The magma chamber is the volcano's lifeblood, housing the molten rock waiting to be erupted. The conduit, or magma pipe, acts as the passageway for magma to travel from the chamber to the surface, while branches of the pipe can create vents on the volcano's sides. The vent at the summit is typically the primary outlet for the magma, with eruptions leading to the accumulation of lava and debris around the vent, eventually leading to the formation of the volcanic mountain we are familiar with.

9.3. Types of Volcanoes

Volcanoes, despite sharing certain fundamentals, manifest in a plethora of forms. The shape and size of a volcano are influenced by the type of magma from which it is born, the rate of eruption, and the geological setting.

Shield volcanoes, named for their gently sloping, shield-like shape, are formed by highly fluid, low-viscosity lava eruptions. An excellent example of this kind is the Mauna Loa in Hawaii.

Stratovolcanoes or composite volcanoes, on the other hand, comprise of alternate layers of lava flows, volcanic ash, and cinders—resulting from highly viscous lava eruptions. Owing to their proclivity for violent eruptions, stratovolcanoes are typically the most deadly. Mount Vesuvius and Mount Saint Helens stand as stark reminders of their destructive potential.

Cinder cone volcanoes are smaller in stature, composed of fragments of lava ejected during explosive eruptions. The magnificent "Paricutín" in Mexico exemplifies this type.

9.4. Volcanic Eruptions and Human Civilization

The dramatic expanse of volcanic phenomena holds far-reaching implications for human civilization. Volcanoes—although destructive—have played an instrumental role in moulding the topography of our world and enriching soil fertility, thus catalyzing agricultural productivity and shaping human settlement and growth patterns.

Volcanoes have also left a significant imprint on mythology and religion, embodying the fury of gods in countless cultures and etching narratives of fear, respect, and reverence in human psyche. Unfortunately, they also bring along colossal catastrophes, as illustrated by legendary eruptions like Krakatoa, Vesuvius, and Mount Saint Helens.

Conversely, volcanoes symbolize potential. Harnessing geothermal energy, as Iceland has commendably accomplished, can pivot us towards a cleaner and more sustainable future.

9.5. Conclusion

As we probe further into the heart of our planet, the role and understanding of volcanoes continue to evolve. They are an eloquent testament to Earth's internal machinations, punctuating our narrative as a species, and continually reshaping our world in both splendid and terrifying ways.

From nurturing life to bringing about ruin, volcanoes—veritable windows into Earth's fiery core—remain an intriguing chapter of Earth's grand geothermal saga. Replete with paradoxes, they inspire fear and admiration in equal measure, proving that even in chaos, there is order, and even in destruction, creation. Volcanoes serve as a reminder of our place in the grand scheme, and the persistence of Earth's transformative nature.

Thus, we invite you to reflect upon volcanoes not merely as agents of imminent danger, but as majestic phenomena that are pivotal to Earth's identity. No matter where we roam, beneath us—is an undying furnace, generating and regenerating existence in its most primal sense.

Chapter 10. The Underworld's Influence: Climate and Weather

Earth's geothermal activity and its influence on climate and weather patterns have fascinated researchers for years. Leveraging both observational studies and intricate simulations, scientists have probed the depths of our planet to interpret this hidden realm's role in shaping our surface world's biomes and meteorological phenomena.

10.1. Unraveling the Subterranean Tapestries

Within the Earth's 6,371 kilometers radius lies an intricate system of layers collectively referred to as 'the underworld.' Structured like a colossal matryoshka doll, the outermost layer is the crust, underlaid successively by the lithosphere, the asthenosphere, the mantle, outer core, and finally the molten core at the center.

From the asthenosphere downwards, temperatures skyrocket to thousands of degrees Celsius, culminating in a blazing core that's hotter than the surface of the Sun. This extreme heat disseminates upwards, triggering profound geothermal phenomena and subtly influencing weather and climate patterns on the surface.

10.2. Geothermal Heat and the Earth's Canvas

In part, geothermal heat determines the Earth's surface temperatures. Directly beneath the crust, heat flux, described as the amount of heat flowing through a given area per unit time, influences the thermal gradient of the upper soil layers. In turn, the surface absorbs and holds onto this heat, bestowing Earth with an ability to maintain a temperature range habitable for diverse life forms.

Indirectly, this subterranean heat also influences the atmosphere. Rising from the Earth's surface, heat shapes atmospheric pressure systems, which drive the trade winds, westerlies, and polar easterlies. These global wind systems play a critical role in distributing warmth across the planet.

10.3. Tectonic Activity: Sculpting Climate Over Eons

As tectonic plates shift, they sometimes enable significant geothermal heat to escape, leading to temporary local climate alterations. But more overwhelmingly, their slow, grinding motions over millions of years have sculpted our planet's continents, dominant biomes, and natural barriers, like mountains, which play an integral role in climate demarcation.

The rise of the Himalayas over millions of years due to tectonic activities, for example, created a rain shadow to its north, engendering the arid climate observed in southern Tibet and the cold desert climate in Ladakh.

10.4. Geysers & Hot Springs: Nature's Weather Vanes

Getting further into the effects of geothermal phenomenons on weather and climate, it's worth mentioning the manifestation of this heat in the form of geysers and hot springs. Often found in volcanic areas, these are essentially nature's hot water heaters, powered by the Earth's geothermal energy.

Enthralling as these phenomena are, they also have subtle effects on local weather patterns. Regular eruptions of geysers, like Old Faithful in Yellowstone National Park, release volumes of steam and hot water into the atmosphere. This injected moisture can influence local humidity levels and may even play a role in the creation of foggy conditions or localized rainfall.

Hot springs, for their part, can also temper local climates. In places like Iceland and Japan, they serve as heat sources during frigid winters, creating microclimates in their proximity that facilitate unique ecosystems.

10.5. The Oceanic Currents: Driven by Heat

Perhaps the most globally significant link between the underworld and the surface world is the mechanism of oceanic thermohaline circulation, a convoluted system also known as the global ocean conveyor belt.

This system, driven by differences in water density caused by fluctuations in temperature and salinity, is vital for redistributing heat around the planet. As warmer water travels from the equator towards the poles, it cools down and sinks, drawing up colder water from the depths to replace it in a continual thermal dance.

While solar radiation powers this conveyor belt, the Earth's geothermal heat subtly adds to the process. At the ocean floor, geothermal heat seeping up from beneath the crust has been found to contribute minorly to this thermal circulation, enhancing the overall heat exchange process.

10.6. In Summary: The Underworld's Weather Wizardry

Altogether, the geothermal phenomena beneath our feet play a subtle yet significant role in shaping our climate and weather patterns. From nudging atmospheric wind systems to sculpting continents, and from painting local weather patterns to driving oceanic currents – the underworld's heat is an unrecognized puppeteer.

Granted, this heat chained deep inside the Earth's mantle does not have a loud and overt voice in weather and climate discussions, often dominated by solar radiation. However, our planet's internal heat is a silent influencer, a quiet wizard, more integral to our climate and weather systems than one might initially realize. Digging beneath the surface, quite literally, helps us understand and appreciate how our atmospherical moods are part and parcel of a larger planetary process that's deeply rooted in Earth's geothermal narrative.

Chapter 11. The Beneficial and Destructive Forces of Earth's Hearth

Geothermal energy, derived from the heart of our planet, operates as a double-edged sword. This ceaseless, subterranean force has the potential to both invigorate our lives, through sustainable power production, and disrupt them, through powerful seismic events. As we delve into the depths of the Earth's core, we will explore how these operational processes are born, and the impacts they can engender, both transformative and catastrophic.

11.1. Origin of Geothermal Energy

The geothermal energy that influences so many aspects of our world originates from two primary sources within the Earth. Firstly, over 45% of this energy has been trapped within our planet since its creation, left over from the high-pressure conditions of its formation.

Secondly, radioactive decay acts as a further contribute to the Earth's internal heat. Specifically, the decay of isotopes such as uranium, thorium, and potassium distribute additional warmth throughout the planet's core. Over billions of years, these isotopes continuously break down and release heat energy, further fueling the Earth's internal furnace.

11.2. Eruptions: Nature's Geothermal Vents

Of the phenomena resulting from the Earth's geothermal energy, volcano eruptions are among the most dramatic. While they certainly showcase the intense power housed beneath our globe's surface, they can also wreak immense havoc. Heat from the Earth's mantle and core rises, melting the crust above into magma. This molten rock collects in magma chambers, exerting tremendous pressure on the surrounding solid rock.

Eventually, the pressure becomes too great, leading to an explosive volcanic eruption. The cooled lava left behind from these eruptions form igneous rocks and volcanic landforms, adding new layers to the Earth's crust.

When observed from a distance, these eruptions captivate with their fiery spectacle, an affirmation of nature's grandiosity. However, on a closer examination, the destruction that trails their wake cannot be ignored. Beyond the apparent losses, i.e., lives claimed, habitats eradicated, and infrastructures shredded, volcanic explosions also mediate long-term impacts. They devastate local economies and can control global weather patterns for years.

11.3. Geysers and Hot Springs: Harnessing the Earth's Steam

Away from the explosiveness of volcanoes, other geothermal phenomena such as geysers and hot springs offer less intimidating showcases of Earth's internal heat. These unique systems occur when water seeping into the crust becomes heated by the geothermal energy below.

In the case of geysers, the water often encounters a source of magma, causing it to rapidly heat and become pressurized. When the pressure is too great, the water and steam erupt from the geyser's opening, creating a spectacular hot-water fountain. Hot springs, on the other hand, do not experience explosive pressures. Instead, the heated water rises slowly to the surface, creating warm, mineral-rich pools.

Both these natural phenomena, aside from being tourist spots, offer significant health benefits. The mineral-rich waters of hot springs are believed to possess therapeutic properties, helping alleviate several ailments ranging from joint pain to skin conditions. Geysers serve as a reminder of the persistent activity beneath Earth's surface, operating like steam valves, releasing built-up subsurface pressure and heat.

11.4. Geothermal Energy Generation: Powering the World

Potentially the most beneficial usage of Earth's geothermal energy is in the production of clean, renewable energy. Geothermal energy plants operate by tapping into the Earth's internal heat, using it to produce steam. This steam then drives turbines connected to generators, creating electricity.

This sturdy and reliable energy source generates power constantly, independent of weather conditions, unlike other renewables such as wind or solar. Furthermore, its renewable nature elevates its appeal, highlighting it as an essential component in the transition towards a clean energy economy.

Despite its promise, unraveling the immense potential of geothermal power is not without challenges. Drilling to access heat reservoirs is expensive, and there are concerns about land usage and possible induced seismic activity. However, advances in technology continue to mitigate these difficulties, bringing us closer to harnessing this magic from the Earth's mantle to a larger, more efficient extent.

11.5. Earthquakes: The Destructive Ripple

Cast against the many benefits of geothermal energy is the unignorably destructive force of earthquakes. They occur when the Earth's tectonic plates collide, separate, or slide past each other, releasing energy stored in the form of seismic waves that ripple across the Earth's surface.

The destructive potential of earthquakes is colossal. They are capable of obliterating entire cities, causing landslides, and tsunami, subsequently creating crises that resonate on a global scale. The correlations between excessive geothermal drilling and induced seismic activity remains a topic of considerable debate and concern within scientific communities.

In conclusion, the geothermal landscape concealed beneath our feet is laden with wonders and threats alike. Our planet's heart pulsates with heat energy that fuels both creation and catastrophe. From shaping landscapes and climate patterns to generating sustainable power, it influences diverse aspects of our existence. As we increase our endeavors to harness this intrinsic vital force, we must refrain from provoking the destructive potential it beholds, for the harmony of our shared habitat depends upon this delicate balance.

Chapter 12. Reflections: The Future of Our Relationship with Earth's Geothermal Phenomena

As we journey deep beneath the surface of Earth, probing the sheer depths of our planet has never been more crucial. The geothermal forces, at once mystifying and formidable, have an imbricable tie with our existence, shaping our world in ways unimaginable.

12.1. Unearthing the Power Beneath Us

The Earth's mantle, brimming with molten rock and blistering temperatures, holds reserves of energy that humankind has barely scratched. It's a ticking powerhouse that has yet to be comprehensively unraveled, even at this pinnacle of technological prowess. As our resources wane, and the need for sustainable power grows more urgent by the day, it is time to direct our quest for energy into the depths of our home planet.

Geothermal energy is harnessed from heat trapped beneath Earth's crust. This natural energy factory works tirelessly, roiling beneath our feet and driving colossal tectonic activity. Fissures and vents form conduits, allowing explosive geysers and hot springs to surface. The surface manifestations of Earth's geothermal phenomena are astounding, yet the concealed power within holds the promise of an alluring future.

With steady advances in technology, we have begun probing the Earth's undulating underbelly, converting its stored thermal energy into power. In places like Iceland, where tectonic activity runs rampant, geothermal energy is not futuristic conjecture but a thriving reality. This new wave of carbon-neutral energy is our beacon of promise in the gloom of our dwindling reserves.

12.2. Geothermal Energy's Potential

The biggest confound that geothermal energy presents is its scalability. Current geothermal projects, while effective, are confined to geologically favorable locations. But what if we could tap into this energy anywhere? What if we could bring geothermal power to places where it's needed the most - large populous cities and industrial centers, disconnected from geothermal hotspots?

Recent advances suggest that this vision may be more within reach than we think. Innovations like Enhanced Geothermal Systems (EGS) have expanded geothermal's horizons, demonstrating the potential for widespread, global distribution. Although still in its formative stages, EGS projects have successfully generated power in locations traditionally considered as non-viable for geothermal energy. Society stands on the brink of a new age; the geothermal age.

12.3. The Roadmap for Globalization of Geothermal Energy

Accomplished as we may be today, the leap from regionalized geothermal energy use to a worldwide adoption cover is undoubtedly steep. It requires substantial research, strategic planning, and robust public-private partnerships.

The globalization of geothermal energy needs a manifold approach. First and foremost, it requires investment in technology and infrastructure. We need drills capable of penetrating deeper into Earth's crust, engineered geothermal systems, and power stations adapted to harness the energy generated.

Furthermore, it also requires overcoming social hindrances. It entails educating the public about geothermal energy, demystifying its processes, and alleviating fears associated with the perceived risks of 'fracking' the Earth.

12.4. Addressing Challenges and Risks

Any significant leap in technology is not without its risks and challenges. Geothermal energy's embrace would require overcoming hurdles, such as instigating seismic activity, ground instability, and concerns of thermal exhaustion. These are real concerns and must be addressed with robust scientific consideration and stringent monitoring.

While seismic risk may be a concern, studies show that the risk is manageable and far lower than naturally occurring seismic activities. Likewise, ground instability has been relatively infrequent with the use of modern drilling techniques, and thermal exhaustion can be mitigated through sustainable management.

Science's role in shaping the future of any society has always been of paramount importance, and it will continue to be the guiding force as we step forth onto this new frontier.

12.5. A Harmonious Future

As we ponder the future of Earth's geothermal phenomena and our interaction with it, it is necessary to cultivate a fine balance. It would be best if we navigated our relationship with Earth delicately, realizing that we're stewards, not masters, of our shared home.

The intricate interplay of untapped geothermal forces and human intervention can lead to an era of harmonious co-existence. This harmonious future with geothermal energy as a stable, reliable power source would not only enrich human civilization but also contribute positively towards global climate change mitigation.

As daunting as the challenges may seem, the possibilities that lie ahead are profoundly exciting. Let us look forward to the future with renewed optimism. The mysteries of Earth's geothermal phenomena invite exploration not just for the lofty ideals of knowledge and curiosity but for survival, sustainability, and benevolent co-existence. Each venture beneath Earth's crust returns as enlightening tales of her geothermal secrets and a glimpse into the future of our relationship with these enigmatic forces.